An Eye on Spiders

# Garden Spiders

by Kristine Spanier

Bullfrog
Books

# Ideas for Parents and Teachers

Bullfrog Books let children practice reading informational text at the earliest reading levels. Repetition, familiar words, and photo labels support early readers.

## Before Reading

- Discuss the cover photo. What does it tell them?

- Look at the picture glossary together. Read and discuss the words.

## Read the Book

- "Walk" through the book and look at the photos. Let the child ask questions. Point out the photo labels.

- Read the book to the child, or have him or her read independently.

## After Reading

- Prompt the child to think more. Ask: Have you seen the web of a garden spider? What more would you like to learn about garden spiders?

Bullfrog Books are published by Jump!
5357 Penn Avenue South
Minneapolis, MN 55419
www.jumplibrary.com

Copyright © 2019 Jump! International copyright reserved in all countries. No part of this book may be reproduced in any form without written permission from the publisher.

Library of Congress Cataloging-in-Publication Data

Names: Spanier, Kristine, author.
Title: Garden spiders / by Kristine Spanier.
Description: Minneapolis, MN : Jump!, Inc., [2018]
Series: An eye on spiders | Includes index.
Audience: Ages 5–8. | Audience: K to grade 3.
Identifiers: LCCN 2017039982 (print)
LCCN 2017046647 (ebook)
ISBN 9781624967917 (ebook)
ISBN 9781624967900 (hardcover : alk. paper)
Subjects: LCSH: Black and yellow garden spider—Juvenile literature.
Spiders—Juvenile literature.
Classification: LCC QL458.42.A7 (ebook)
LCC QL458.42.A7 S625 2018 (print) | DDC 595.4/4—dc23
LC record available at https://lccn.loc.gov/2017039982

Editor: Jenna Trnka
Book Designer: Molly Ballanger

Photo Credits: Musat/iStock, cover; Meister Photos/Shutterstock, 1; Schroptschop/iStock, 3; JillLang/iStock, 4, 23tr; redtbird02/Shutterstock, 5; NHPA/Photoshot, 6–7, 23tl; BLANCHOT Philippe/hemis.fr/Getty, 8, 23br; Sari Oneal/Shutterstock, 9; CathyKeifer/iStock, 10–11, 20–21; Brian Gordon Green/National Geographic/Getty, 12–13, 23mr; Maria de Bruyn/Shutterstock, 14–15; Rocket Photos/Shutterstock, 16–17; Eric Isselee/Shutterstock 18, 22, 23ml; Darkworx/Dreamstime, 19, 23bl; Osote/iStock, 24.

Printed in the United States of America at Corporate Graphics in North Mankato, Minnesota.

# Table of Contents

# A Good Catch

Spin! Spin!

A garden spider spins a web.

It starts in the middle.

It moves out.

The web is big. It is round.

A garden spider has claws.
They help spin the web.

claw

**Look!**

**This web has zigzags.**

zigzags

**Why?**

**So birds won't fly into it.**

9

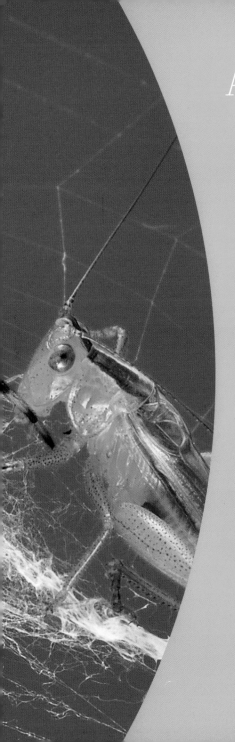

An insect is in the web.
Good catch!

Garden spiders
have venom.

It kills the prey.

Time to eat!

13

Where do garden
spiders live?

In sunny areas.

They are yellow
and black.

Their legs are
orange and black.

Baby spiders hatch in fall.

They stay in the egg sac all winter.

egg sac

They leave in spring.
They build their own webs.

19

They catch their own prey.
Good job!

# Where in the World?

There are many kinds of garden spiders. They are found throughout the world in areas with warm weather. They prefer to live around plants, flowers, and sunshine.

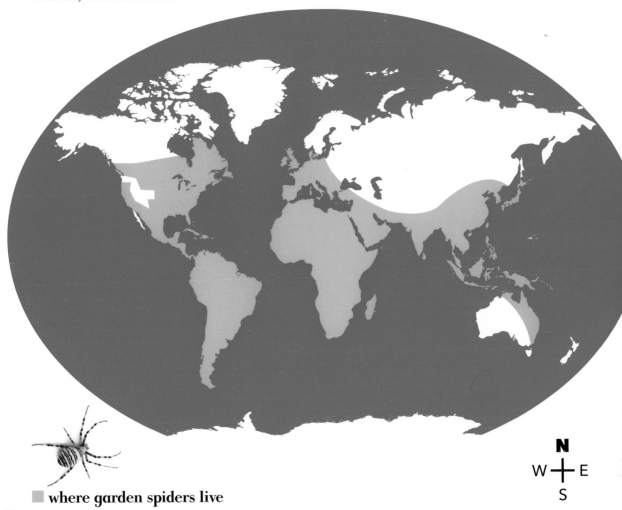

where garden spiders live

# Picture Glossary

**claws**
Sharp, hooked structures on the legs of a spider.

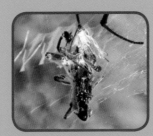
**prey**
An animal that is hunted by another animal for food.

**egg sac**
A protective pouch in which a female spider lays her eggs.

**venom**
A poisonous substance spiders inject to kill prey.

**hatch**
To emerge from an egg.

**zigzags**
Lines that move from side to side with sharp turns.

# Index

# To Learn More

Learning more is as easy as 1, 2, 3.

1) Go to www.factsurfer.com

2) Enter "gardenspiders" into the search box.

3) Click the "Surf" button to see a list of websites.

With factsurfer.com, finding more information is just a click away.